TO

SEE

YOURSELF

AS

YOU

VANISH

TO SEE YOURSELF AS YOU VANISH

Poems

Andrea
Werblin
Reid

Wesleyan University Press
Middletown, Connecticut

Wesleyan University Press

Middletown CT 06459

www.wesleyan.edu/wespress

© Estate of Andrea Werblin Reid

All artwork by Bensley and Dipré

All rights reserved

Manufactured in the United States of America

Designed by Mindy Basinger Hill

Typeset in Adobe Jenson Pro

Library of Congress Cataloging-in-Publication Data

Names: Werblin, Andrea author

Title: To see yourself as you vanish : poems / Andrea Werblin Reid.

Description: Middletown, Connecticut : Wesleyan University Press, 2025. |

Summary: "A posthumous collection describing the poet's experience facing terminal
    ovarian cancer; a heartbreaking work of witness as Reid reckons through verse
    with the pain and beauty at the end of life" — Provided by publisher.

Identifiers: LCCN 2025019704 (print) | LCCN 2025019705 (ebook) |
    ISBN 9780819502070 cloth | ISBN 9780819502087 ebook

Subjects: LCSH: Cancer--Poetry | LCGFT: Poetry

Classification: LCC PS3573.E6 T6 2025 (print) | LCC PS3573.E6 (ebook) |
    DDC 811/.54—dc23/eng/20250515

LC record available at https://lccn.loc.gov/2025019704

LC ebook record available at https://lccn.loc.gov/2025019705

5   4   3   2   1

CONTENTS

TO

SEE

YOURSELF

AS

YOU

VANISH

LIFESPAN

for every denim summer of mistaken rage,
hurtful choices dissolving your own best interests,
certain fates were meted out accordingly. it felt fair.

now is the age of illness as a crime you can't stop
committing. now you author shrines to good health.

now daffodils are a construct hinging on melancholy.
daffodils strutting lately in your living room, struggling
without vague snow to defy.

now is the age a surgical knife can be a hero,
cowboy cancer to save you from madness.
and for a while it works. it works for a while.

DISTENDED

decades ago the swell in your belly
might have been something worthy
of celebration, mapped inextricably
to your heart. a draft of you. a becoming.

now the form imprisons. pings away time
differently. now it fills in with danger.

now you're trying to get this all down,
the details inside the gap, every chapped lip,
trial, ambiguous gesture. radiator's incarcerated hiss.

and those other thoughts become charming,
middle-aged blushes. pink as baby skin.

TUGBOAT CAPTAIN

once you agree to the prognosis, what becomes of your crystal-balled
    ambition?
will you lose the elastic evergreen of longing? will you be able to—
    even once—
try to reason that your life before might not actually be the better one?
droll darkness notwithstanding, you are an insipid biography of yourself.
kind and generous, you continue, maneuvering with every pitch and yaw.

no one to tell you how it all turns out, but then that's how it's always been.
disease or not. so now maybe you get a closer peek at the ending. so what?
it's not like there's some exotic gathering you're missing out on.

it's just you and this thing. this floral now. this ochre-colored where do i begin?
please stop paperweighting your errors in judgment; these misdeeds
will no longer serve you. think what it might look like—even once—

not to make this into a movie. not to crave a rescue, wings, ports, or harbors,
not to consider yourself overboard.

ASSURANCE

like a swing set remembering giddy up-and-downs,
or mud recalling the stomp of rubber boots,
you think long and often about a soft, safe feeling.

what right do you have to wake up unannoyed,
as though nothing is glitching inside you, as though
the trauma your cells experience is essentially a lie?

it's one of the universe's favorite tricks:
to percolate, then slip in as you go about your day
awake but not alert, steady but about to tumble.

you have a right to feel bad, they say. it's okay
to be angry, like you were looking to them
instead of the scornful wallpaper for permission.

nobody is wrong, remember? whatever decides
which bodies may grow older and which must
chronically walk on wire to eke out a few more years
—is like everyone else, barely managing
to squeak by its own caustic revelations.

LANGUAGE IS A VIRUS

the first rule of fight metaphors is there are no fight metaphors.
the second is, will you just stop kidding yourselves? it's not like
you didn't already know how to be insufferable pilgrims
radiant with judgment. they say *she lost her battle with*—
like it was a duel she entered at dawn, like she was ever
in possession of a pistol. there is no *fight against*.
there is *live with*, for as long as humanly possible. and that's another thing
    i think you
ought to examine, why some lives are more salt-in-the-wound than breath
on the beard of an iris. there is the solitary devil of her disease.
there are swing sets, volcanoes, the time she hurt her foot
tripping over rocks near the river. how about mineral then?
how about saying, *she has gone to the quarry, having found*
the dolomite of her dreams? having found the perfect shade
of ochre? to die is not to lose. survive is not akin to conquer. as for
    guarantees, there
aren't any anyway, only sonnets
and foxes and the memory of her crinkly hand on the doorknob.
she didn't fail at being human, at least i don't think she did
but who am i, who are we, each of us excruciatingly mortal.

LETTER TO A TORSO

dear what-is-left-of-my-almighty-iridescent abdomen,
how do we reconcile this hotbed of unknowing?
how do we feed it better? right now we are pills
by the staircase and meds in the fruit bowl labeled
hazardous, labeled *caution: may cause dizziness.*

all you want is to mother the body into cooperating
with the brain. for the brain to go out on a limb,
and for the two of them to rise to power
—*cymbals clashing!*—and begin a kind of healing,

to let healing be something that comes *from* you
instead of something done *to* you. to refuse all
overcast days. to illustrate fire in the chemotherapeutic
margins of your treatment, or be a simple fountain
receiving coins and wishes, in service of yourself.

THE COLOR OF WAITING

is hypnotic pink, under whose spell
you've been living for years
like a small fossilized creature.

or magenta, a bruise
that evolves, so you must
continue to adjust your secrets.

waiting is rosy, a soft-spun
medical soundtrack of static
frizz, machine screech

then sharp as the serrated smiles
doctors have been honing for years.

waiting masquerades as the inflatable idea
of hope, waterproofed for safety, maybe,
devoid of vision, punctured that easily.

A.K.A.

chemo erases your fingerprints and this feels almost like a perk,
like cosmic approval for a life of crime. through phone lines
you can feel people backing away. you the human reminder
of flaws and mortality. no one is meant to be an atlas.
it's unfair to put that kind of pressure on a person, whoever or whatever
you think they'll become: the famous wind with its many appointments,
insatiable mosquito, or noiseless spider scaling furniture, thinking—
for once—not of spinning intricate webs, but of freedom.

WOLF MONTH

they will say that cancer spared the husband
only to come back for the wife. they will say,
cells replicate like this all the time, it is January,
when wolves come starving to the village.
hunger makes them bolder. It isn't when but how
they will take you: in sleep? hope you are that lucky.
they are more ravenous than their future widows
pacing the salted lip of streets. watch for
the upside-down blackbird. feel the unharbored wind.

RE-TREATING

in your mind it feels like this: you walk into a hospital and
a bridge explodes. a face flinches from a hand. a man walks out of a bottle.
    somewhere else birds call out in a sound so grave and divine, it divides
sunset, which was otherwise busy blazing across the wide neckline of the sky.

SORRY SORRY

how many times will you make people say it,
even if none of this is their fault?
human language offers few less-awkward options.

is this the straw that breaks the cancer's back?
because the cancer's back, it turns out.
turns out to be embers, not ash. like some jerk
leaving a campfire to die or catch again—

hissing into brambles: you cannot face this again,
though you will face this again,
numb as you make yourself, human as the poison is.

CONTEXT

at first the rug being pulled out
from under knocked you breathless.
now slipping is familiar as air
in this way you are transformed.

when disease says *transform*
what it means is *inure*.
and *fire* means turn on a *dime*.

when it says *choose,* it means slip
into the underworld
whistling a brook of conundrums

but rarely, if ever, says *choose.*

THE WORLD OF THE WELL

my feeling on this is *whatwhatwhatwhatwhat* so i guess my feeling is a
    helicopter. plus fury. plus, who decided to divvy up our world this way to
    begin with?

if it makes you more comfortable, by all means, monkey things in two:
one a hideous alien landscape, the other, tadpoles dreaming lily pads.

and if you see me sweating in Target from the simple act of reaching
for a box of noodles, my head in a wool cap in the middle of summer
because i don't believe in head wraps, go ahead, stare in order to separate us.

stare and draw the line. just know when i stick out my tongue in reply
    (i will) i am basically saying: you might have it too. a dodgy cell waiting
    to go rogue.

or one already rogue blooming deep inside you until it becomes a tower
    of rules and needles and prescriptions that will not be ignored. you
    think i'm joking.

if on a lark it decides to take you, it will—slowly, unpleasantly,
until you are but a powerless sketch in your teenager's notebook,
a secret told behind your own back, a parable of shattering buttons.

TRANSFORMERS

hope shape-shifts into sadness with mere vibration,
so it should be vice versa, yet there you are
on a hospital table considering the clay wingspan
of winter with its *what ifs* and *maybes*
polka-dotting air. the dream of making wings
with only a stick of glue is elemental
like the need for glass, for something somehow
to refract rays of light, so you have the option
of regarding your life as more than a mythic flash,
so you can convince the soon-to-wither blossoms
on your dining room table that they make
an actual difference, when almost nothing else does.

MENTAL

for the record, please state your name and anxiety,
the reason for your glassy eyes, and why
your apartment is immersed in slices of light
when all you do is speak of their opposite:
brute storms and guards, nightmares
that cheat their way through.

it's not where the brain meets its bully,
remember how the synapses are salted.

it's just regular thoughts gone turntable
a series of nouns maimed as they exit your mouth.

please state your pills, the state of your lungs,
the stripes of every zebra you remember.

if machines don't work, there is always
umbrage, altars, u-turns, you could try gratitude
sure, but that's a different kind of singing.

DRIVING WHILE GRATEFUL

the ogre of gratitude dangling like a chandelier from the rearview mirror
asks if you know how lucky you are, if you've meditated on that yet,
   if your heart

is as full as true practitioners agree it should be? oh yes, absolutely
yes, you want to answer, so much you can barely contain it.

and yet: if cherries with their dark flesh are a blessing, for example,
so is the indulgence of asking what's next. because who knows?

from the ashtrayed turns this life has given you, maybe an empire.
from your wild heart, a reckless slumber, now that treatment is over,

your skin hangs in a symphony of corn husks, your eyes pie-widen
in the chronic search of something simpler: a doodle, a seed,

a borrowed cup of sugar, a chunk of moonstone as ancient
as the moon itself. It's hard, we hear you. the one day a month

you get to drive and everything feels dangerous, the cars ahead,
behind, the policeman directing traffic in the rain.

even the gravel is suspect. the sound of mercy skidding to a halt.

BETRAY

whoever insists staying positive is—
let me stop you there, let me tell you about
this ugly algorithm that brought us all together.

rogue cells, a cowboy cell, that one cell
that fucked up everything—
it's a useless mythology: neat but absurd.

don't think about *cured*, she said. think about *healed*,
because cured is an island and healed is like—what?
a burning sunflower?

hope is the most ridiculous option on the table.
it's a silent creeper, sweet-veined rosebud offering up
pinpricks of light. i wouldn't let that in if i were you.
there's nothing innocent about it.

ONLINE SUPPORT GROUP

don't keep going there; the news is mostly terrible.
freckled laments about life as it was, as it could be,
cottage *this* and tragic traffic circle *that*.
and of course, questions about baldness.

where can a person go then in search of
charitable cyclones and untwisted ropes
of conversation?

what counts as a gift here changes as often
as the weather, from flaky croissant
to confetti-ed lampshade to the cardinal
you're sure is your father.

look at them in their folding chairs
resigned to the ceiling fan's hum, worrying
over mutations and wholeness.

O, my wounded berries, i'm sure this empathy for us is
mostly kindness sponsored
by gravity and a passionate shade of red.

before tending to all the bodies grounded
first be certain they want to get up.

EVIDENCE FOR THE ROLE
OF MINDFULNESS IN CANCER

to represent the trouble of savoring every moment
of every day while wishing they'd all be lies, begin
with the image of a rescued tiger, fierce but blind,
blind and dizzy. like you, seeking sanctuary
from some terrible circus. meanwhile, the pressure
to embrace every droplet of rain on your tongue,
every childhood friend who ever climbed trees with you.

it is not a choice to avoid comfort but an understanding
that there is no actual rescue. how is there peace in the moment
when what you see is moments pacing, showing their teeth.

TRYING TO MEDITATE

each day you wake wishing that what is, is not, and that's no way to live.

even the doctors with their glassy words will tell you: trust the dark

coming on early in winter, even if it sounds ominous for your life

in its current state, even if it feels like the very sun being severed. trust
    nighttime. but that other lurking—the elephant not just

in the room but every human corner—is suspect.

adore it, they say, *like the ancient puzzle it so clearly is.* that's fine

for fables and koans but you are so through with tests of every kind,

even the ones that don't require a needle to access your port. the world asks
    so much of you, as though you are its daughter.

even as it yells and yells at you coming up the driveway,

replaying all your errors and nightmares in its hatchet voice,

you keep hoping it still loves you in a way you can't yet see.

THE WORDLESSNESS OF FIXED TIME
& SIMPLE BLESSINGS

you decide to live by assumptions: you can duct-tape

the earthquake waiting at the back of your throat by applying

lipstick the color of cosmos that a cosmos might survive the winter.

assume that even if the solar system blackens and divides,

it will reassemble, inoculated. assume that a ribbon of particles

and energy can become a roadmap in the sky. assume

roadmaps. through the cancerous minefield the world lays at your feet,

assume no flooding or despair. assume with every plundering rock

you can contrive a necklace of pearl.

EXPECTANCY

the owl refuses to dispense any wisdom
but has a few questions of its own:

what exactly is your elegant emergency?
the wrench in your otherwise outstanding plan?

the owl's eyes are neon. The tree he inhabits
so lovely & upright & full of its own spine

it is almost unbearable. so sure of its roots.
don't ask how much time you have left.

ask if you are fully enjoying your tiny house
of secrets & sacred truths, because you know

we all betray ourselves somewhere. don't ask
about years. ask what any animal is thinking

as it becomes the owl's dinner. ask about the blur,
the sudden shrinking view of outer space

you see while on your back in a musty tent,
the ceiling of which has been cut into

to allow some windows of sky.

STARGAZER

all summer, they've been inching closer.
during the solstice, for the first time
since the Middle Ages, Jupiter and Saturn will align.

a bright planetary flash in the sky, which seems
to you a wild thing. which makes you think
it means something more than just what it is.
but this is what planets do.

the timing just a coincidence. like the way
both you and your father were diagnosed
the same year. a conjunction is all.

planets aren't like you, reckless in their movement,
nor so riddled with nostalgia.
there's some mystery, sure, but it's you

who tries to make things into paper stories.
you who need the myth that somehow something
up there could really affect anything down here.

that a rare happening in the hallways of night sky
can somehow make curable your certain absence.
restore your plush existence.
so stop embarrassing yourself. science has no feelings
about disease one way or another. a conjunction is all it is.

the planets had nothing to do with it.

LAST FULL MOON OF THE YEAR 2020

your fatal flaw was thinking the universe didn't have one,
believing it was anything more than a black, codified expanse
made to lift you up like a pendant.

depleted arsenal notwithstanding, you are still a tenant
of the grass, able to skid with delight across divine, iced-over lakes.

like everyone else, a collage of tendons, caverns, and knots,
a curious valentine to outer space, not knowing which angles
prove your devotion, how hard you should love in order to live.

YOUR STUPID IGNORANT BEAUTIFUL SELF
IN THE TIME BEFORE EVERYTHING HAPPENED

thinking about teeth and lemons and the art of macarons, which are still too
   fancy for you:
oh, i'll travel. i will luxuriate on islands, seduced by fatigue and the geometry of
   coconuts.
thinking, *no rush on that.* thinking you'll love some particular song for the
   sake of the song,
for radical enjoyment, reading nothing into its lyrics of talismans and dark
   times. *oh man,*
that's folk music for you, am i right? said without irony.

now you get a sense of just-around-the-corner, just-around-a-pocket-door, a
sense of pushing it, though the old wood sticks and swells in summer heat. if
you push it hard, you see: a tin replica of life as it used to be, once was—cool
as linen, patiently waiting. a sense of, *just walk in and take it back,* knowing
everyone on the inside will pretend this with you, they will, they'll say
they've never heard of two such outrageous things together in the same
   sentence!
you, silly you, and deadly cancer. they will say *let's go on as we were, as you*
   were.

you can't imagine how possible this seems, even as you know it is next to
   nothing.
to reach back like that, to reclaim—so easy it takes only gesture, takes one
   small,
staunch step, so possible that feeling, byzantine in cruelty, so true in
   intention you
can't help but admire how whole the ache.

AT LEAST FOR TODAY

they say live in moments as though
that is a thing people actually manage

to do, as though your future is not
a trick but a humming lake to be circled,

and you've recently felt its song as barricade,
its water a green quilt of ceremonious calm

you could slip right under. Understand?
even if the lake is tumor and trap, the future
a useless drink, you find you must sing

your diamond horoscope out of its box.
you must put on your stubborn coat and hum the way.

THE FLORA, THE IMPOSSIBILITY

we learn as a people to ditch daffodils
the second their petals brown or
as soon as the vase water looks gray.

gone their credentials as symbols,
hope defying winter, summoning
excitement for a sunnier season.

because the moment something starts dying
it is no longer living is how the logic goes.
how the logic goes is, in the middle of writing,
the hospital calls about your latest drug, something
to keep you from dying while you are living.

this isn't a treatise on the beauty of dying
(which seems mostly to exist in poems anyway)
but a thought on brevity, the contradiction.

the logic goes that a creature cannot be dying and living
at once, except in certain cases: fuzzy bugs half-squished
beneath the wheels of your childhood bike. you admit
you thrilled sometimes at their struggle, and now it is yours.

now you must take that drug, try to be alive while dying.
you do not have the credentials to be a symbol of anything
auspicious, and nothing is spelled out clearly.

PATIENT

first, are you medically sound?
has your brain become a titanium doodle
or a gently spiraling machine?

because what we're hearing you say is
you try to stay positive, forge a skylight
into your darkness and we're sorry but
no one believes you. we're sorry
but there's just no way—

you for whom they're stopping treatment.
you with one lung. you whose tumors grew
while waiting for a hospital bed during a pandemic.

where we come from the galaxy's just a bunch of junk
with a few patches illuminated by prayer.
whether preserved with painkillers or camouflaged
by chamomile, anger is not an impediment to the picture.

we're not saying it well but what we're saying
is for the love of god will you please just
scream it out? we are with you in the rawness.

we support your jagged edges from the inside out
only good can come of it, we know this, once
escaped from the trap of your body it is limitless,
almost criminal, all that outrage turned tenderness.

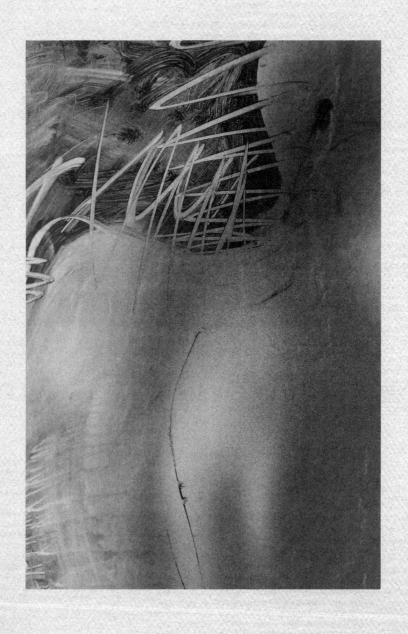

CLINICAL TRIAL

In exchange for a public chance at a longer private life, you give them,
not your body, but your body's one error in calculation. the swerve,
detour, blunder unique to your system. you give them the soft scribble
of your consent. in exchange for a future where you might run
among penguins, or consider the altitude of a lark, his small brown body
racing vertically into the sky, you agree to be watched like a hawk.

Asked hundreds of times if you're ok, if there's anything they can get you.
longer life most people think. *glass of water* most people say,
since there is often some small thing lodged in the throat.
you remember that larks sing when they fly, unlike any other bird.

RIVALS

the logjam of appointments you grandmother
without grace, the easier to eradicate later

the ceiling mosaic you memorize
lying on the shed floor, peach in one
lazy hand, mason jar in the other

they are so many sirens now, the full dozy summers
make them incarnate, make them less real,

that way you have of making
the doctor into a glass partition
who stands before you
and knows before you

how long before your true hold might loosen

who knows before you
what counts as irregular
and senses as you leave
the hint of vinegar in your voice

WHAT WAS THAT GAME CALLED?

the one where you woke in the middle of the night
and could not move your hands? the doctors called it
immune response. the Dictionary of Dreams
called for balance. and for absence: said part of each day
you should now consider the proximity of your own funeral,
the ghost shapes of zinnia and snapdragon.
and part of each summer that you are alive,
consider time ferrying over beaches and cliffs
to arrive at rhinestone sand.
overheard: i do not want to leave this skyline.
overheard in your head.

PLAIN OKAY

for Lisa

how to return to the world its breath
gorgeous with sweet peas
and the history of sweet peas,

to return with your ghosts
absorbed or in exile. how to go,
ears more open

to the harsh ascending sermon
of redwings. return without policing
the body. how to say now

you're okay, minus all grief's
parentheses: okay (for a person with
cancer), (for a fatherless child),

okay
(for a person talking
in circles, scratching at air).

RECKONING

don't dangle that laundry metaphor in front of me one more time—
the business of disease is dirtier than you imagine. its language

is organized to blame the body, which does not fail treatments but is failed
    by them.
which is not a brave soldier but the battleground it falls asleep on,

it spent most of its life avoiding crowds
and parties and still was not immune.
if my particular illness spreads as they say
it will, like dandelion seeds, tell me

who is the one to make such a sinister wish,
to take a breath, and blow?

this is only one tale, where weeds
keep weeding. in truth there are others
with open windows, bluer days
anticipating something

small and pinned back,
cautious, but good again. allowing room,
a future right now you cannot enter.

YOU GET NO EXTRA POINTS FOR MAKING IT THROUGH YOUR MORNING SHOWER WITHOUT NEEDING TO STOP AND SIT DOWN

each stubborn hoop begets another, and that's what you're talking about,
the alabaster nature of disease, unerasable by prayer & fleecy moons
& gnawing down on the yellow of your no. 2 pencil until it isn't a pencil
but a synonym, until it is the creepy mental line you drew last year,
to determine your level of hope. it is balm and burden, just so many
needles drawing fluid off your abdomen, the nurse who does it expertly
& the doctor who causes pain. it is immune to visionaries though
they may say otherwise. it signifies bent sunflowers, uneven things,
luck askew, and you without the wherewithal to draw it again, or the interest.

INSOMNIA

siblings, sutures, and sandpaper tongues, we are all pre-existing conditions,
which is enough to keep even the doziest of people awake
for what seems like ages, but which is actually just this past year and a half.

the kleptocrat whines in his translucent enclosure.
his squirrels gloat in tandem, proceed with frenetic grace.
there is no opting out of this drama.

plus you have your own unchangeables: a nearing proximity
to death, for example, your astringent transformation into someone
who believes she can refuse it.

as for life being fair, what's new there? people die or worse every day
for any reason you can imagine. mothers blanked from their children's
memories. children who will never get to meet themselves.

as for mercy—mercy is a tour guide newly bewildered at every comer.
an axe, an ache, a scant memory. a perpetual cleft in the system.

PLAN

I spy with my drugged-out eyes a wooden ship
sailing the hospital halls, an animal on board with roses
'round its neck, has a message:

I am a particle or a wave or both—am light misbehaving.
a dogwood, I cut myself down to the ground in winter

then grow back from the buds at the base. ambidextrous,
I writhe both left and right and I will never hibernate
or try to curate miracles in the absence of a fitting god.
I know science wouldn't let me anyway—

but how else to pass on the message—that I am
still thirsty in the world, that parts of me are raw knots
working themselves out, demanding a better shape
than the one I'm currently in? how to get it through
the world's thick skull that being a temporary, roving energy
is not enough, at least not now, while there are still roots
and porticos with harmless animals peeking through,
gliding down hospital aisles, making me believe things.

THINGS DISEASE HAS TO TEACH

1. You are a well-loved iceberg, nonetheless
cast off, and you float somewhere the skies

are perpetually white, the snow raining
fitfully like ash, from nowhere in general.

2. *hospital yawn* is a thing, choreographed
from hours of waiting to be read a different story.

it doesn't tend to diminish. 3. also perpetually
white: the starched sequential sheets.

with their pristine folds, in obedient order.
meant to be a kind of calyx? for me,

who keeps forgetting the meaning of *flutter*.
is that snow the kind that's good for making snowmen?

4. You have an affinity for snowmen. 5. in this life
you are a poseur, a poster for well-hidden health.

now that my hair has grown back, no one
can tell from looking at me. 6. the idea

there is anything like rescue is a bottle bobbing
about the ocean with its cliched letter inside,

the handwriting stretched like hunger,
7. an absent tongue.

YOU SAY *LATE* LIKE IT'S
A BAD THING

1.

afterwards, they'll call you *late*
like you are really just having
one of those days—burnt-toast,
traffic-jam late—and you will
for sure show up anytime soon.
but you will be late to the party.

2.

the bumper sticker on the car
in front of you says it's *never*
too late to have a happy childhood,
one of those linoleum lies doctors
told patients in the '80s. in any case
you have always been a late bloomer.

3.

a day late and a dollar short describes
the bluster of treatments they offer you.
but you know your way around
a thunderstorm now, stay up too late
watching the storm clouds roll in.

4.

now sometimes late in the day
you will get up from your desk
to watch the sun sink over snow.
bare trees keep their mouths shut.
they have been doing that lately.

PEOPLE FIND IT DIFFICULT
TO TALK ABOUT CANCER

every good intention you are left with clings exquisitely to its branch,
a plain owl in his marvel of upright sleep, a joy to have witnessed
his arrival to the tree. hollow that way, each perspective.

each sentence leveraging the wish that more could be done
to make you better, omits the lofty ending, *for as long as possible until*

as it is, people will keep telling a dying person to *stay strong*
right up until the moment her soul and body separate,
so what good, in certain conditions, is language at all?

when someone asks what it was, what caused it,
what could they personally avoid not to get it themselves,
you say *bad luck*. avoid bad luck if you can, because that's what it was
and that's what it is and mostly nobody wants to hear that out loud.

THINGS I DON'T KNOW HOW
TO TALK ABOUT ANYMORE

maybe the power that made the body can heal the body
or maybe it's all just physics and secrets in the sand,

who knows anymore? maybe running out of options
would push anyone to the brim of a bad decision.

now the world softens a little and starts to open
but only in certain corners. now you make a contract

with yourself. even though there are knots where
your notes should be, even though the cadence

of thought runs angry, with awkward lulls and hums.
you agree you will somehow heal yourself from the inside

because the outside has gotten too hazardous.
because you used to think you could recoup

everything from your one clandestine life:
friends, paintings, frail fragrances, wood and wire,

wholesome and trash, the real and the substitute—but now you know.

CHARM

thank you my friend for the gift of scarabs to ward off evil,
but honestly that ship has already left the harbor.

I say this not from the depths of a depressive episode
but from a sliver of wise mind, from the peaceful center.

if there is another alphabet to turn to, I'd like to know it.
the one i have now, though vivid, is what they used

to spell my diagnosis, so those are the letters i live by.
besides, there's hardly a need for talismans when truth is

anyone can be perfectly fine one day and terminal the next.
what brand of starlight is *that*? which aurora's particles were charged

with that decision? just as celestial objects come and go from view
in the night sky, diseases decide their visibility. there's not much

more to it than that, despite the language of warriors and battles.
which is not to say you shouldn't charge at it with everything,

stand what you can stand, hang your hat on the slim ratio of stars.
but don't trust too much in amulets or inklings or resolve, prayers

placed on bird wings or in the house of your chosen lord—
there's no proof they have bearing on a cell gone rogue, by definition

a loner out for blood. measure out gratitude with yardsticks
and hope you are dead wrong.

PORT, THE DEFINITION

a vehicle embedded above your breast,
opposite your heart. from which blood is drawn
and into which various liquids enter, only
some of them poisonous. an opening.
a passageway. a maritime facility, pretty
as a postcard, the place where charming boats
arrive after their adventures. a haven.
the left side of a ship, when looking forward.
a drink of sweet, fortified wine.

if you are lucky enough to arrive at the third year
of a beast, does the beast become your lifestyle?
become a new galaxy, dyed hospital-beige,
with beloved words turned upside-down gems?
portable, portrait, portrayal, portend, all of this.

SNOW DAY

all afternoon you keep your head beneath a blanket,
asking every unanswerable question of the stupid world:
why most people's speech is half ashes, half grackle,
how whole futures morph in the blink of a cell, and why,
given that you've tried your entire life to be good,
there is no sufficient reason for a body to trouble itself with disease.
nothing to explain how disease chooses which body.

all night you keep looking out the window for signs.
a neon snowman lights up a neighbor's driveway as an offering.
you are asked to trudge unknowing through
this terminal inconvenience. going forward now can only be
by whim or folly. or by blindfold, the dark thing trilling.

WHEN TO RESIGN

when to sew up the frantic pockets
currently designing your life, when
to decide to farewell. how long to keep
scolding your generous body, trapped
as she is between liquid fatigue, scalding
blue antiseptic, and simple tremors of sun:
like a lake full of yellow-flag iris.
like a future swarming with plans.
when to stop toying with determination,
its toxic stem of hope. when is it called
just being realistic when your brave face
loses power before a mirror? so many do.

YOU KNOW HOW THIS ENDS

of all the emotions a doomed person might have,
one I did not expect was disappointment—not at the world
for letting me down (it did), but for taking away so soon

the delirious mystery of my finale, death's declarative *tra-la-la,*
the thrusting pelvis and pivoting heels, making us second-guess
what would happen the entire time. how weirdly boring in a way,

to know the *what,* even if not the actual *when.*
was I looking forward to its erratic pace and shiver,
the unraveling of the unknowing, a delicacy in a delicious dream?

maybe I was just looking forward to the surprise:
would it be on a bicycle against a backdrop of sunbeams,
or in a sympathetic lap, rain beating at the windows?

I never planned on trying to declare victory at the last possible
second (who could?), but it had been kind of nice
to think about, how my singular ruinous daydream

in ending, would come to life.

NEW YEAR'S ABSOLUTION

now that the mystery of your ending
has been all but decided, the prospect
of hope is a false, grave fancy.

trust me: you will puncture every morning
trying to solve the criminal fog and madness
of your childhood. at the crossroad of gravity
and glittering proof is a long silver thread
you will follow like a clue, leading not
to transformation but repetition—

which scares you most.
knowing personally how hope brings
people to their knees.

METASTASIS

grief is an apple, with many varieties, only some
in season. the lush catalog of absences
you live with now plus nostalgia
for healthier cells. where winter holds
its hostages: the driveway under ice, the woodpecker
who goes on pecking anyway because it can.
the magic of the disappearing friends is
harder to believe than you might have imagined,
harder to swallow, even had you been able
to imagine the sword of all this,
even had you found comfort in the labyrinth,
joy in the exile, trust in the first tart slice.

SPIDERS & MARS

tonight will be giddy with moons: full moon, blue moon,
moon of Halloween, all held hostage by a bright red Mars.

you should know, blue moons aren't actually blue, but the hawk
who landed on your deck that time actually was a hawk.

or else it was your late father, having finally found his footing.
or an omen of future unfriendings. a messenger from God.

maybe one of the moons is a pizza pie, another a tincture,
an elegant electrician of the darkest skies. the hawk is at least believable.

the question is which myths hold you hostage, and which ones
will you let carry you to sleep? Mars has no face and no ocean.

you have your vowels and revolution. insects swarm your telescope
like protesting colonels, threatening to mask every sparkler you can see.

WALDEN

there in the pond her soul is swimming
still attached to earth, all freckles, moss and neon swimsuit.

and the cicadas going at it, the heaviness of her human puzzle
still unsolved, the turn to ghostly matters.

it's bad enough isn't it, with her earthly body mostly ashes, limbs long gone?
no one enjoys these pictures but there is no sleeping

without them. stories like heavy wings. her soul

stroking, in its old, odd ways.

stop attaching everything
to something else. how much
for this exercise in sadness,

how much
does it weigh, what
does it cost you
to keep it hidden?

SOMEONE ELSE YOU KNOW
GETS CANCER

you want to tell her there is no god to ask,
there is only her body as stranger, only mean luck
and that familiar feeling, that—animal, vegetable, mineral
—we are all succumbing to something.

which is another way to say the universe wasn't really
holding us up to begin with. tell her considering her mortality
every day for years will leave her eyes glazed and spirit locked,
spirit busy keeping score with her body. and as for living
her original allotted amount, maybe yes, maybe no, maybe
chance fells her life expertly like a tree, or fells a different tree,
and moves on.

consider this is mostly geologic anyway, embedded in the solid matter
of celestial bodies, so she may as well plead her case to the tongue-tied
    moon.
tell her what you thought was god was only a constant hum.

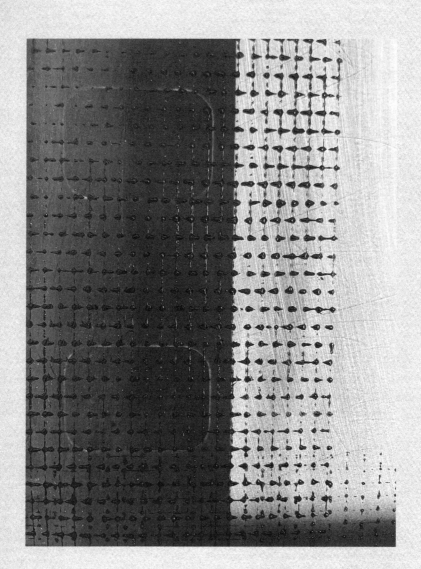

THE JEOPARDY OF YOUR THINKING

when you are gone, who will climb
the steeper staircase
to pardon his wild hands in sleep?

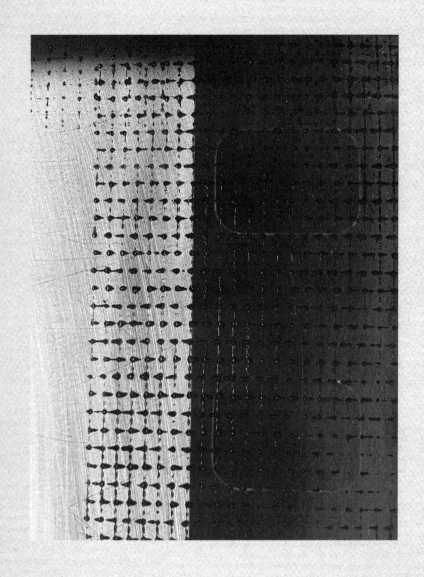

APPENDAGES

you just go along now like it's normal, the rogue cells and random patterns,
but once you were the moth, knitting its way through every hanging garden:
moonflower, petunia, evening primrose. once you were the stubborn shrub.
you alone decided when to flower. now your skin is dry as crepe paper,
your pelvis mostly hollow. now you have a contract with some afterlife
or intelligence, something mystical to hope for, hang onto.

if forces guide you toward darkness. would you go there?
if it came to plunging the charcoal depths ever so slowly,
like a brittle starfish, would you?

KINDS OF RESISTANCE

to not accept the fact that your life
has been cut short takes more energy
than you might think. not that you'd
necessarily think about it, but if you did
just know it's exhausting. if you are out there
fighting for a different kind of justice
disappearing
even if the certain death hanging above you
feels more chandelier than starless black,
it is no less certain. you might see your face
suspended in glass prisms, but that is
the only difference i can think of, that
you'd be able to see yourself as you vanish.

LOGICAL DISJUNCTION

either you can allow for a way this might turn out differently, or you can't.
either you welcome the left hook its knuckle bones deliver,
or risk messing with the proverbial monkey who is on his mark,
getting ready. please don't try to deviate; it's exhausting.

the silent ritual you sometimes observe is either blessing or bitch—
it's hard to tell sometimes, because the whole time
you are circling the devil's inseam, the rouge is leaving the rocks.

something is diminishing. choose either clean ocean amplified
or dusty road endured, no in-between, no finish line.

acceptance is a blatant foreign flower. either you deign to
what people call its beauty, or keep trying
to wrest the steering wheel in the direction you mean it to go.

HOW TO GET UNSTUCK

the trick is not to envy the apocalypse
its sudden vacuum. not to fiddle,
but note how the wild irises bloom and crash,
bloom and crash, until it's clear there's
only one particular magic you should care about.

the trick is, keep your vowels safe
and your sorries homespun. the root of why
you can't turn, why you obstacle every waking moment,
has more to do with bitterness than disease.

anger is not a keepsake nor trouble a starry invention:
staying still is the crime your father left you:
an unsullen sideways gaze that never quite commits

to being instrument or enemy, or innocent,
wholesome thought. his albatross of spirit.

ONCE UPON A RIDICULOUS COUPLE OF YEARS

the marigolds swell with yellow. the t-shirt elopes with the spoon.
the battle-axe princess in her fuzzy tower is quelled by dust.
for these fables and more you are grateful.

adage of the apple notwithstanding, you recite your luck
each night before sleep: to live in the time of cyborgs,
the privilege to prioritize linen, a wealth of oysters waiting
in McMansions, thank you, O universe, for this age.

and for love, doctors, really good medical insurance.
dusk settling over your backyard like lace. frail pipes
that croon through every fuzzy hour of your being.

how long can you keep this up? selfishness is the Cadillac
in the room, and with all due respect, there's that lot
you're not as thrilled with: the shitty deal you feel you've been given,
the lack of justice in this fractured world, memories that get harder
to recall, turn sour by the minute, like fables coming up on the truth.

KEEP LIVING

days are drums & echoes
of drums, & sometimes

you hear the animal crescendo
of someone else's final days.

all living tissue feels like flattery.
like earth serenading the after-earth.

& sometimes you walk metaphorically
of course, to the rim of something vulgar,

to peer over. it's human to constantly measure
that arc. nights are wings & imprints of wings

& sometimes you embroider in your sleep
the caves of every place you meant to travel.

PEOPLE SPEAK OF THE FUTURE

when you say you'll retire in Boca Raton
your backyard fat with the children of your children,
know your audience. know the sound of your plans
crackles across frequencies like static and hurt.
its outreach is fuzzy at best. know there are colorless voices
in the yard you are forbidden, on ordinary Sundays, to hear.

prayers plagiarized from laurel trees
and sticky hibiscus tongues. stylized metaphors
sung by cardinals in the back alleys of this blissful earth.

when you near your ending, you'll know what i mean.
propping up your elbows on the windowsill,
searching for luck, knowing luck has little to offer.

ADDRESS

untethered, unterrestrial, amidst the lakes of stars—if no longer in the
    purposeful,
painful human space,
where do you live?

among peonies and porch breezes. in the opening of a cupboard, the creak of a
stairway. an early bird trill. In empty passenger seats, where we ask you for
    advice,
and in the violet minutes ticking time every time we wait in line.

you live in every difficult decision. by cool creeks, along highways and in
long, questioning gazes at waxing moons.

you live in us because you are us. we don't know where you are, but we know
where you live. you are home.

HEREAFTER

you don't know for a fact that the sky is benevolent,
you really don't. in a superstitious world, in the loaming,
while planets appear as gumdrops, the dead peer through
ceramic twilight cutouts. they could be anything.

calling them stars is simplistic, but kind: if you ever need me,
just look up, says the terminal young mother to her infant son.
it gets you every time, though the truth is his tiny memory
blurs by the hour. so maybe not stars. they have enough going on,

seriously. science says that given the opportunity, stars will suck
the life from planets and eventually explode. so, not as romantic

as you'd thought. if not stars then quotation marks, surely.
punctuation as a guide to the afterlife. choose what helps you sleep.

because what if the dead turn out to be not extraordinary energy
circumnavigating the universe, but ordinary, kitchen-corner dust?

eventually you agree to grief's permanent, loose handshake.
your anger evolves, and bumblebees leave their drunken
drowsy autographs all over the summer garden.

THE DAZZLING ODDS

knowing what you know, the scuttle
that finally breaks you is not the image
of your partner blinking at your empty
kitchen chair, remembering pancake sundays,
but the genuine epiphany of your own absence—
radiators still thumping through winter,
black ice still marking the roads.
with the motor of you missing,

not knowing what you can't know,
do not deprive yourself of the chance
that some stream is already rising.
some neon light burning in the body
dares to untether itself, and waits
at the juncture of *here* and *not here*.

not even science knows everything,
what you're certain is rust in one light
is easily ornament in another.
believe you'll live beyond expectation.
amplify the thought inside you.

HOW TO TELL THE DIFFERENCE BETWEEN A RAVEN, A CROW, AND A TIRED BODY

something something corvid. they are all dark birds calling.
An unkindness of one, murder of another. with practice
you can tell them apart: lazy ravens ride the thermals
their tails like wedges. crows do more flapping.

the body brandishes a fist at them both from their position
on the orange couch. it is trying to take its mind off
certain poisons, which have their own kind of claws.

the raven has a commanding croak. the crow can purr
like an idling engine. the body is just tired in a way
the birds don't understand. no matter—they all caw

anyway 'til they're blue in the throat, feeling like omens
one bird comes to the end of his branch looking like a clever moustache
one bird comes to the end of his song looking like an ordinary bird.

COMPACT

agree to live beneath the owl's stony stare

and continue the scant attraction to living.

let it cease to be even scant.

sometimes a chorus of painkillers will save you

and sometimes it will be your own enchantment with the world,

the world as a field of baffled daisies. hold fast to the myth

of the blackbird and the golden cosmic egg, ignoring when possible sutures,
scars,

symbols of the body's necessary impoliteness.

trust something as simple as a string might tie it all together.

let a handful of wings take hold.

WHEN YOU'RE DONE

when you're done being angry, we don't want to hear about it.

when you're done being tired, sarcastic, forgiving, and bitter—

done with rabbit holes, chakras, and mantras of cruelty—

when you're done with all the dang stories of your life unspooling

like polite paper wings. when you get near to collapsing, finish

with catapulting wrongs and the disorder of street maps.

when you finally release the cluster of fossils you hold fast to,

place your brain into orbit like a twinkling satellite,

then you will be welcomed. tugged on constantly by the gravity

of earth, freed to take advantage of its rotation.

UNDERTOW

voice like a floral pillbox, whispering in the rain: *come forward,*
just a little. leap, as though into the Grand Canyon, it says,
and you will be emancipated, finally, from disease and its famous affiliations,
from these nail-biting, doom-scrolling, rosary-holding October evenings.

before voting with vision and passion, collaborating in the aftermath,
and reclaiming what little gravity has been left, please consider soil.
the idea of becoming understory, it is just one floor to fall,
one stubborn perch to yield, one vision not as innocent as it looks,
and then there you are, silk-like, grass, exempt from explanation.

ACKNOWLEDGMENTS

Andi, a lifelong poet, stopped writing after her initial diagnosis. She hated the idea of being a "cancer poet," and cancer was taking over her life and ability to think about anything else. Her dear friend and fellow poet Debra Gregerman encouraged her to join Aliki Barnstone's daily online writing group, where she slowly found herself able to write again, and the floodgates were opened. Enormous gratitude to them both and to Dale Tegman, Christina Hutchins, Cynthia Hogue, Lindsey Royce, Jacob Griffin Hall, Liana Sakelliou, Deanna Benjamin, Elisabeth Frost, Karen Brennan, Yasmeen Mir, Shelly Norris, Stephanie Kartalopoulos, Nancy Sherman, Agnes Vojta, Molly McKasson Morgan, Lisa Rhoades, and to the others who dropped in during this time. Your close-knit gatherings were a reciprocal lifeline and the key to Andi's return to poetry. Thank you for your sustaining faith in the power of language and for attending this work with open ears and hearts. All these poems exist today due to the love of this group.

To the medical team of Dr. Megan Shea, Kimberly Maurer, and Teri Forbush for their care in Andi's last years and to a dear friend, Christine McCarthy, who helped her navigate her final days with dignity and peace.

To the Virginia Thurston Healing Garden, especially Brianne Carter, Christine Zinke, and Erin Raber: Thank you for providing community and care when Andi (and I) needed it most. The reaction to early drafts from the staff and patients here, seeing that her writing could help a little, set the direction and goals of the work.

To Anne Tonachel: Thank you for your special care and for encouraging Andi to read for the women at the Turning the Tide Ovarian Cancer Retreat. Her final reading was a triumph of defiance and humor, and getting her to it is among my finest moments. Thank you to Melissa Tonachel for recording that reading and to the women who attended subsequent retreats. Andi would love nothing more than to know you gather for a poetry workshop and begin with a reading of her work. You are the reason she finished this collection, and she would want to read every word you write.

To Daniel Pritchard: Thank you for decades of close friendship, collaboration, early reads, and for so generously supporting publicity efforts for this book.

To Melanie Bishop: Thank you for your eagle-eyed reading of early manuscripts and support in publication and promotion efforts big and small. We can always count on you to lend a hand and catch details we might have overlooked. We are so grateful for your friendship, support, and sharing of skill and talent.

To Melissa Maerz: Thank you so much for your appreciation of Andi's work and your kindness and support as we moved toward publication.

To Beth Bishop: You answered a last-minute plea to help shape a pile of poems into a book. Working under a ridiculously tight deadline and with incredible sensitivity for Andi's journey—and the readers'—you got us where we needed to be. We couldn't have done it without you.

To Suzanna Tamminen, director and editor-in-chief at Wesleyan University Press: Thank you for diving into this book with wisdom and passion. We are so grateful for your expert edits, sequencing of poems, and your deep sensitivity to Andi's work, having known her since you were both junior publishing nerds at your first professional conference and working so closely with her while editing her first book.

To Nicola Bensley and David Dipré: Thank you for your generous collaboration and gorgeous artwork. Especially the photo on our cover about which Anne says, "As someone who has lived with ovarian cancer for twenty years and spends much time with other women who have it, this cover is a stunning representation about how some of us feel about our bodies as we live with ovarian cancer. I keep going back to it and am moved every time." The rest of us are moved too. Thank you.

To Rob McQuilken: Thank you for recognizing the power of Andi's poetry, taking her book on, and growing it into what it is today. You have done so with such deep sensitivity for her and those who love her. You have our heartfelt and eternal gratitude.

To Sarah Sawyer: For loving Andi, being an early reader, finding Rob, working on edits and pagination, meeting with publishers, managing our publicity and social media, and generally picking up this work back when it was the bulky, disordered, fragmented grimoire she called her "Stupid Cancer Poems" and running like the blazes with it when I was destroyed and had no idea what to do or who to turn to.

To Joe Strummer: Andi was madder than hell most of the time while writing this book and nothing expressed that like *London Calling* turned up loud.

—G.R.

ARTWORK BY BENSLEY AND DIPRÉ

ABOUT THE AUTHOR

Andrea Werblin Reid (1965–2022) is the author of *Lullaby for One Fist* (Wesleyan University Press, 2001) and *Sunday with the Sound Turned Off* (Lost Horse Press, 2014). She was a finalist for the *Missouri Review's* Perkoff Prize, and her work has been published in the *LA Review of Books*, *Virginia Quarterly Review*, *Massachusetts Review*, *Brooklyn Rain*, *Pank*, *Smartish Pace*, and elsewhere.

Andrea, Andi to her friends, grew up in Boston and settled there, close to her beloved sister, Lisa, and their parents Barbara and Marshall. She also lived in Tucson, Arizona; Sandpoint, Idaho; and Barcelona, Spain. In Puerto Rico, at the wedding of two friends, she met Gus Reid: a kind, funny Scotsman who would, after a transatlantic courtship, become her husband. Before her death she entrusted Gus with her literary estate, and he has shepherded this work to publication with great love and devotion.